Into the Black Box: Observing Classrooms

Geographical
Association

Photo: Margaret Roberts, Department of Educational Studies, University of Sheffield.

Theory INTO Practice

Into the Black Box: Observing Classrooms

SHEILA KING

PROFESSIONAL DEVELOPMENT FOR GEOGRAPHY TEACHERS

Series editors: Mary Biddulph and Graham Butt

Geographical
Association

The author
Sheila King is Lecturer in Education at the Institute of Education, University of London.

The series editors
Dr Mary Biddulph is Lecturer in Geography Education in the School of Education, University of Nottingham and Dr Graham Butt is Senior Lecturer in Geographical Education in the School of Education, University of Birmingham.

ISBN 1 899085 82 3
First published 2000
Impression number 10 9 8 7 6 5 4 3 2 1
Year 2003 2002 2001 2000

Published by the Geographical Association, 160 Solly Street, Sheffield S1 4BF. The Geographical Association is a registered charity: no 313129.

The Publications Officer of the GA would be happy to hear from other potential authors who have ideas for geography books. You may contact the Officer via the GA at the address above. The views expressed in this publication are those of the author and do not necessarily represent those of the Geographical Association.

Designed by Ledgard Jepson Limited
Printed and bound by Colorcraft Ltd, Hong Kong

Contents

Photo: Sheila King, Institute of Education.

Editors' preface

Theory into Practice is dedicated to improving both teaching and learning in geography. The over-riding element in the series is direct communication with the classroom practitioner about current research in geographical education and how this relates to classroom practice. Geography teachers from across the professional spectrum will be able to access research findings on particular issues which they can then relate to their own particular context.

How to use this series

This series also has a number of other concerns. First, we seek to achieve the further professional development of geography teachers and their departments. Second, each book is intended to support teachers' thinking about key aspects of teaching and learning in geography and encourages them to reconsider these in the light of research findings. Third, we hope to reinvigorate the debate about how to teach geography and to give teachers the support and encouragement to revisit essential questions, such as:

- Why am I teaching this topic?
- Why am I teaching it in this way?
- Is there a more enjoyable/challenging/interesting/successful way to teach this?
- What are the students learning?
- How are they learning?
- Why are they learning?

This list is by no means exhaustive and there are many other key questions which geography teachers can and should ask. However, the ideas discussed and issues raised in this series provide a framework for thinking about practice. Fourth, each book should offer teachers of geography a vehicle within which they can improve the quality of teaching and learning in their subject; and an opportunity to arm themselves with the new understandings about geography and geographical education. With this information teachers can challenge current assumptions about the nature of the subject in schools. The intended outcome is to support geography teachers in becoming part of the teaching and learning debate. Finally, the series aims to make classroom practitioners feel better informed about their own practice through consideration of, and reflection upon, the research into what they do best - teach geography.

Mary Biddulph and Graham Butt
January 2000

Introduction

Even in an educational world of increased openness and scrutiny, classrooms are still largely the private domain of the teacher. Many long-serving teachers have taught upwards of 40,000 lessons with only a handful observed by other adults. However, classroom observation is becoming increasingly common. Teacher appraisal, novice teacher supervision and increased research into classroom processes have led to a wider scrutiny of classroom practice.

If a lesson is worth observing it should be worth analysing properly. Most teachers would not wish an observer to leave their lesson with a vague comment such as 'Thanks. That was a good lesson'. They would rather have an opportunity to discuss the context and the outcomes of the lesson in a detailed and useful way.

Observation should be an integral part of teaching. We can all learn from watching each other no matter how long we have been teaching. This book examines the contexts, purposes and types of observation, together with their uses. Skilled observation can ultimately raise standards for everyone in the classroom; informing and improving the quality of the activity. Observation without purpose or without sensitive, intelligent analysis, can rightly be resisted by staff who become hostile to the whole observation process.

Recent developments in education have led to schools becoming more committed to school effectiveness and improvement. Such developments include the introduction of the revised national curriculum, publication of performance tables and Ofsted inspection cycles, and the increased autonomy of schools through Local Management of Schools and the Standards Fund. Schools now see themselves as pro-active in self-improvement. As part of this complex process, systematic, professional observation work is being used to inform the work of teachers, departments and schools. It is my belief that classroom observation will become a more integral and accepted process, used regularly by all teachers.

Several useful texts advocate reasons for, and describe techniques used in, observing classrooms, including: Wragg (1999), Tilstone (1998) and Adelman and Walker (1976). This book draws on such research and gives a concise general background to the issues surrounding classroom observation. It then focuses on the ways in which geography teachers and other professionals can benefit from observation practice. Chapter 1 examines some of the practicalities necessary before embarking on any observation work. Chapter 2 describes observation techniques which are useful to any teacher. More specialised, geography-related observations are then discussed in Chapter 3, although teachers of other subjects and the humanities in particular will be able to adapt some sections for their own use. Chapter 4 addresses the reasons why experienced teachers will find themselves undertaking classroom observation. Finally the video lessons, which can be purchased as additional materials to accompany this book, are described in Chapter 5.

Who should engage in classroom observation?

The short answer to this question is all teachers, at all stages of their careers. However, in reality observation is most frequently practised by:

- Novice teachers
- Newly-qualified teachers
- Mentors observing novice teachers
- Initial teacher training tutors observing novice teachers
- Appraisers
- Teachers engaged in action research
- Local education authority and Ofsted inspectors.

It is hoped that this book will encourage more teachers to build regular, focused observation into their work and through so doing raise their standards of teaching and the levels of their students' achievement. Forward-looking geography departments will find that observations, formally scheduled into the year and discussed at subsequent departmental meetings, will highlight best practice and provide data for raising standards and improving the department as a whole.

It is important that agreement on the observer's role is reached with the class teacher before the lesson takes place.
Photo: Sheila King, Institute of Education.

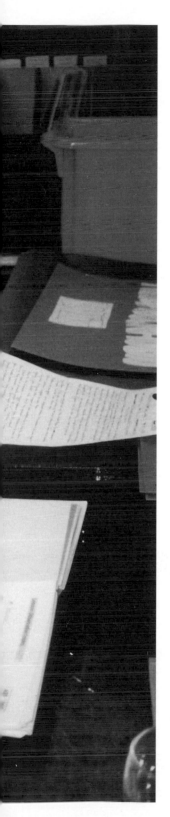

1: Classroom observation techniques

Working with the class teacher

It may seem an obvious point but before observation takes place it is essential to seek the agreement of the class teacher and to discuss the process. Details of the task, the focus and methodology for observation should be discussed in addition to the time and location of the lesson, and how any feedback will take place. It is important to remember that the ethical foundations of classroom observations are founded upon two issues: firstly, the informed consent by the participants and agreed access to the classroom and, secondly, the appropriate use of information gained from the observation (Barnard, 1998).

Whether students know the observer or not, it is likely that as the lesson progresses they will ask the observer for help with their work or want to talk about what they are doing. It is usually desirable that the observer does not participate in the 'life of the classroom' and this may need to be explained to the class in advance. Any observer, whether known by students or not, is likely to influence what goes on. (Newly-qualified teachers may find their lessons abnormally quiet and well behaved when the Head of Faculty observes the lesson.) Generally, the more 'open' the classroom and the more students are used to having unknown observers in their lessons, the less the observer will influence the usual atmosphere.

Sometimes the observer will benefit from joining in activities and talking to students during the lesson. This is referred to as *participant observation* as opposed to an observer playing no part in the lesson, or *non-participant observation* (see Tilstone, 1998, p. 63; Wragg, 1999, p. 15). Figure 1 is a case study of Jenny, a newly-qualified teacher who used observation as one strategy to improve her understanding of teaching physical geography. During the observation time, she needed to discuss students' understanding of their work on glaciation, therefore some interaction with them was necessary. It is essential that agreement on the observer's role is reached with the classroom teacher before the lesson takes place.

Figure 1: Case study of a newly-qualified teacher's observation to improve her teaching of glaciation.

Jenny was a newly-qualified teacher (NQT) working in Kings Langton Comprehensive School. Recognising that her knowledge of physical geography needed improving, she arranged, through the NQT mentoring tutor at the school, to spend (limited) time working with an experienced geography teacher.

After a discussion with the teacher about the strategies she was adopting to teach glaciation to a GCSE class, Jenny arranged two lessons for observation, two weeks apart. She saw how the teacher put across difficult terminology and concepts and discussed with students what they were finding straightforward, more difficult, helpful to their understanding and interesting about the work.

A further discussion with the teacher, after the unit was completed, built on the observation experience. Finally, Jenny was able to compile a list of ideas which she could use to inform her own work and which she shared with the teacher and her mentor. Jenny was also asked to report back at a subsequent faculty meeting so that other teachers could benefit.

Jenny's findings included:
- Geographers use a complex vocabulary. Ask students to keep a glossary at the back of their exercise books and regularly check students' understanding of terms covered earlier in the year. Cards could be made as new vocabulary arises with the term on one side and the meaning on the other. They could then be put into a class box and 'dipped into' at the ends of lessons to reinforce learning.

- Visual images through slides, video or photographs help students to see and understand complex physical processes and landforms.

- Students learn by doing, so episodes of lessons should include students talking about what they have learnt (e.g. in pairs, students explain different processes to their partner. Noisy, but constructively so!)

- Students need to know content for examinations so use homework for them to learn and then be tested on the work. Reinforce and revisit concepts.

- Try to avoid students copying out diagrams. Most students find this easy but feel they learn little. Teacher (or students) could cut and stick diagrams into their book ready for labelling in later lessons.

- The rules for skills work need to be reinforced each time the skills are used.

Observers familiar to the school may find it difficult to detach themselves from what is going on in the classroom. They may teach some of the students or have already formed beliefs and prejudices about the class, the teacher or the lesson objectives. Unfamiliar observers, while more detached, may take longer to relax into the environment and may misinterpret events.

The observer must be sensitive to the feelings of the observed teacher during the observation and also in any post lesson discussion. Few teachers enjoy being observed. Many feel threatened by observation and perform less effectively. Observers with a higher status than the classroom teacher should take care not to use this to affect the students or teacher. The pre-lesson discussion, when the observation objectives are being outlined, is an opportunity to help the classroom teacher feel more relaxed about the process.

When novice teachers observe experienced teachers' lessons the observation process is rather different. This often takes place in the early weeks of the course when novice teachers are getting to grips with the multi-dimensional, changeable and busy places that classrooms tend to be. When novice and experienced teachers do not know each other very well the novice will need help to make best use of the process. Any outcomes of the observation will need to be discussed and handled sensitively during feedback to the class teacher, if the novice teacher is going to be able to analyse them effectively. Novice teachers should be encouraged to avoid making assumptions about the teacher's thinking and actions. They should make notes of questions that they wish to ask the teacher and about the situations to which they refer.

Recording observations

Observations can be recorded in various ways. Teachers wishing to research a particular aspect of classroom life often use pro-formas to structure their work. Several pro-formas are included here as exemplars - but observers are also encouraged to adapt or create their own versions which fit the exact purpose of their observation.

Novice and newly-qualified teachers are entitled to written as well as oral feedback. Written feedback can take a variety of forms from pre-drawn pro-formas to unstructured, hand-written notes. Wragg et al. (1996) found that 75 per cent of 1000 teachers questioned who were involved in appraisal used freehand notes to record their observations. The observer is then challenged to draw key points from these ad hoc statements and to focus points for future action. Many institutions responsible for initial teacher training have a standard observation sheet with predetermined headings, often printed on self-carbonating triplicate sheets. This enables observers to give a copy to the novice teacher, file a copy with the school and keep a copy for themselves.

Written accounts can be descriptive or evaluative. Novice teachers often use descriptive accounts when they observe a more experienced teacher's lesson and to help to focus questions about what went on in the lesson. Descriptive observation notes might look like this:

> 10.28 Desks rearranged into groups before the bell. Students lined up outside – greeted and asked to enter. Stood behind desks and sat down quietly. Register taken and then recap on last week's lesson followed by objectives (written on board earlier) of today's lesson. (Do you always take register at beginning of lesson? Is this always the best time?)
>
> 10.37 Discussion of what makes Burton the same as some towns and different from others. Students thought of many appropriate answers as well as a few silly ones. They engaged well with the activity and were keen to answer and to listen to other students' ideas. The boys near the window took very little interest or part in the activity. (Did you notice?)

Evaluative accounts concentrate on the quality of what is observed. The same part of the lesson described above may be recorded as:

> Main focus for lesson = what students are learning.
> Very good pre-lesson preparation and classroom organisation.
> Students greeted and brought into lesson well.
> Register taken effectively although it took considerable time. (Could this have been done once students were on task?)
> Recap on last lesson effective although you could have asked the students to tell you more answers. Objectives for this lesson were clear and well addressed.
> Discussion on Gateshead went very well with most but not all students taking part. (Which group did not?) You managed to quash silly replies and to praise thoughtful examples very well. I thought this was an episode which really made students think and gained their attention. (It is a pity you didn't encourage the girl who mentioned McDonald's in Moscow to expand.)

Figure 2: Recording observations: advantages and disadvantages of different approaches. Adapted from: Wragg, 1999.

Method	Advantages	Disadvantages
Written account	Immediate and fresh account available; economic use of time; account may be available immediately after lesson; full picture of events available to observer at time of observation.	Observer must make immediate decisions about what to record, so account may be superficial or unreliable; no chance of 'action replay'; some effects on class behaviour because of observer's presence.
Video cassette	Good visual and sound recording which can be replayed several times; no pressure to make instant decisions; focus can be on teacher only or on individual or a group of lessons; lesson can be discussed with participants watching.	Loss of information such as events out of camera shot, smells and temperature; effects on class of presence of camera; increase in time needed for analysis.
Audio cassette	Good sound record can be replayed several times for discussion, analysis, or corroboration of written account; radio microphone can be used to obtain high quality record of what the teacher says; observer's comments can be recorded simultaneously on twin-track tape; allows lesson to be transcribed by audio typist.	Loss of important visual cues such as facial expression, gestures, body language, movement; sound quality can be poor without radio microphone, especially if acoustics are poor; difficult to identify individual children who speak; analysis time substantially increased.
Transcript	Enables really detailed analysis at leisure; permits analysis by several people not necessarily in the same place as text can be distributed easily; person being observed can work on specific aspects of language, such as choosing good examples of analogies, using appropriate vocabulary.	Loss of important visual and sound cues such as tone of voice, volume of noise, emphasis; high cost in time and money to have lessons transcribed (one lesson might fill twenty or thirty pages); difficulty of deciding what to focus on if numerous transcripts are collected.

Many observers find a mixture of description and evaluation to be a natural way of presenting their thoughts. Whatever method is chosen the main purpose(s) of the observation needs to be clear in the observer's mind. This allows targets to be set, progress to be monitored and a more systematic approach to 'learning to teach' to take place. Observers can comment using a number of predetermined headings such as preparation, pace and timing, or they can focus on one or two aspects of the lesson, as agreed previously with the novice teachers.

Most of the observations described here are recorded through a written account. Sound and video recordings with or without a transcript may be more thorough and give more detail, particularly for research purposes. Figure 2, adapted from Wragg (1999), summarises the advantages and disadvantages of each type.

The observation debrief

Whether observers are debriefing a novice teacher, a member of their department or a deputy head, the debrief must be handled professionally and with sensitivity. Teachers live constantly with the notion of 'failure' as well as 'success'. Because of the unpredictability, fragility and multi-dimensional nature of classrooms the actual outcomes of many lessons often do not meet the planned outcomes. Classroom 'failures' are public, particularly when an observer is present.

Some immediate feedback should be given even if brief. The quality of discussion is important. Many teachers' opening remarks after an observation begin with statements such as 'Was that OK?' or 'Sorry, that didn't go quite to plan' or 'That was a bit boring wasn't it?' Observers frequently begin with 'That was fine' or 'Well done, that went well.' Such comments must be followed up further.

Detailed discussion of the lesson findings with the teacher is a matter of courtesy but should also provide further information to add to the observation notes. The conversation may take place later that day or the next, since the observer or observed may need to rush off to another part of the school to teach. This pressure on time can lead to an observer simply handing over the written notes to the teacher with a comment about arranging a discussion later. Such notes rarely tell the whole story and to be most effective they do need to be explained and elaborated upon. This debrief is also a useful way to help less experienced teachers develop their ability to reflect and evaluate their lessons. Figure 3 offers guidance for effective debriefs. Some observers shrink from raising issues while others attack with judgements that may be over hasty and achieve little. Achieving a balanced feedback is crucial.

Some able novice and newly-qualified teachers are insufficiently challenged towards the end of their teaching practice or during the first year of teaching and should be encouraged to reflect on alternative teaching techniques and strategies. Although many teachers are preoccupied with the 'performance' and delivery of the lesson, the main focus of most observation work should be 'what are the students learning?' and 'how effectively are they learning?'

Figure 3: The effective debrief. Adapted from: Institute of Education, 1999; Smyth, 1991; University of Birmingham, 1998b.

Timing and environment

Debriefs are best done on the same day as the lesson or the next day if this cannot be arranged.

An informal and friendly atmosphere should be created, away from interruptions and eavesdroppers.

Observers should be aware of body language and show sensitivity to the observed. They should bring in their own weaknesses and anecdotes to avoid appearing to be the model teacher.

Describe	What did you do during the lesson? The observer can also describe what has been seen or experienced in the lesson from his or her perspective.
Inform	What pleased you about the lesson? What did it mean – to the students, to you? What do you think the students learnt in that lesson? How do you know? The observer can also offer his or her perspective on this.
Confront	How did you come to do it (plan it) like that?
Reconstruct	How could you do things differently? Are there alternative ways?

Structuring the debrief

Observers should focus on:
- the teacher's successes or achievements in the classroom
- the action taken by the teacher to achieve those things
- the teacher's reasons for taking the action he or she did.

Observers should generally avoid:
- a generalised question such as 'Do you always introduce the topic in that way?'
- closed questions, in which you attempt to test your own ideas, e.g. ' Did you cut short the question and answer session because you thought you were getting confused?'; 'Can you tell me why you cut short the question and answer session?' is likely to produce a more illuminating response.
- moving on to the next question too quickly. Don't be afraid of saying 'Could you tell me a little more about that?'
- asking 'Why didn't you ...?'as this puts teachers on the defensive and leads them to justify their teaching rather than to reveal their thinking.

At some point, time should be spent in analysing the debrief and feedback. The following questions should be considered:

- Who does the talking? Mainly you? Mainly the student? Shared?
- What are the benefits of doing most of the talking yourself? What are the disadvantages?
- What are the advantages of verbal compared with written feedback?
- What are the advantages of written feedback?
- Is the discussion focused on targets and target settings?

Adapted from: University of Birmingham, 1998a, p. 37.

Ethical implications

Davies (1985) argues that the consent of students (and their parents) should be sought before an observer gathers data in a classroom. This, he believes, is an ethical issue rarely considered by classroom observers. Some schools are now writing and issuing policy documents including statements to parents that cover the purpose of observation work and the circumstances under which observations are likely to take place.

School **managers** involved in observation processes need to consider the following points:
- Class disruption should be minimised during observations.
- Care must be taken that one group of students is not over-observed.
- Teachers should not be overloaded with observations at inappropriate times.
- The way external observers are perceived; whether they are seen as valued consultants, welcome guests or tiresome gatecrashers.
- Teachers and management should also gain advantage from any external observers' work.

Classroom **observers** need to be:
- very well briefed about the purpose and management of their observation work;
- clear about their involvement with students, participant or non-participant; and
- aware that their chosen methods of recording e.g. stop watch or video camera, may have an abnormal effect on the behaviour of the students.

Finally, **teachers** and **learners** should be:
- clearly informed about the purpose of the visitor;
- aware that the visitor may alter the normal character of the classroom; and
- active in deriving any benefit from the observation debrief.

Photo: Richard Greenhill

2: Approaches to classroom observation

Although this book discusses observation within the field of geography education, there are many approaches to observation that are common to all classrooms. More detailed methodology about common approaches can be found in Wragg (1999), Tilstone (1998), Acheson and Gall (1980) and Stubbs and Delamount (1976).

Quantitative or qualitative observations?

Quantitative methods follow a 'scientific' or positivistic approach. Conclusions from such research usually focus on significant statistics that challenge or back up our existing ideas. Examples from a selection of studies show that on average teachers allow only one second between a student's answer and their own statement (Rowe, 1972); that 57 per cent of primary teachers' questions were related to classroom management, 35 per cent to information recall and only 8 per cent to high order thinking; and that teachers can engage in over 1000 interpersonal transactions in one day (Wragg, 1999). Wragg writes that:

> '... at the heart of the quantitative approach is a belief that the effectiveness of teachers can be improved if a body of knowledge is established which shows that they should do more of some things and less of others' (Wragg, 1999, p. 9).

Some examples of quantitative methods which have been adapted for use with individual classes or groups of students are given later in this chapter.

Qualitative methods loosely follow an anthropological or ethnographic methodology. They encourage observers to detach themselves from the familiar and to probe into events to interpret and explain their significance. Data collection takes into account not only what the students do but also the environment, the context of the observation and the interaction with the teacher and other students. Results of qualitative studies can be found in Wragg (1984), King (1978) and Delamont (1976).

The type of observation methodology and techniques chosen will be determined by the reasons for carrying out the work. This chapter offers a range of different approaches. Readers are invited to digest the examples given and to produce their own methodologies guided by their intended research or observation foci.

Observing classrooms holistically

The first approach to understanding classrooms as a whole is based on the concept of the ecosystem. This approach is especially accessible and relevant to geography teachers who take an integrated or holistic approach to understanding environments outside the classroom.

Classrooms are busy, multi-dimensional, unpredictable and complex places. Some teachers who enter the classroom after a break of many years find that by focusing on one aspect at a time they gradually build up a picture of the whole classroom environment. Other teachers find it more helpful to observe a classroom holistically from the beginning, viewing the classroom as a whole and then studying particular aspects. One analogy of the holistic approach is making a walking tour of a city before deciding which areas to return to and study in detail. An alternative image is of the observer viewing through a wide-angle lens compared to a zoom lens.

One attempt to help holistic observers begin to unravel classroom complexities is a model based on the concept of an ecosystem and developed by Doyle (1977) and Lambert and Sankey (1994). Figure 4 relates the biological model to the classroom analogy. It suggests that as an observer develops from a novice to an experienced teacher, the greater the degree of complexity within the classroom that he or she can understand. Figure 5 presents six categories that form the basis of the model and can be used as a focus for discussion in almost any classroom. The observer is asked to write notes on six categories and to decide questions or issues that should form the basis for the third column.

Use of this model requires substantial creative and intellectual input from the observer. Only a limited number of responses can be made at each observation and not all categories can be completed at the same time. Joint observation and subsequent discussion by novice teachers have been particularly useful in this work. Extracts from the work of one geography novice teacher demonstrate the outcome of this type of observation.

> 'I think the most important feature of the class was how strong the unit seemed ... energy seemed to have been harnessed by encouraging the novice teachers to be independent learners, by allowing them freedom to move around, to use resources on the walls or to start up the computer ...Using an understanding of the ecosystem model it is clear that one of the most important aspects of this class is its history of long established practices and routine.'

One strength of the model, she went on to write, is that it, 'helps to direct and guide observation, breaking down complexities that are too unmanageable to be dealt with initially as a whole'.

Professional development	Categories	Biological model	Classroom analogy
There is more to classrooms than meets the eye. To accept this is an essential prerequisite of the beginning teacher. For you, all classrooms have existed before you enter them.	• not self-evident • but given	The processes which underlie, say, a rainforest ecosystem are not obvious. Not until the concept of a system was imposed did an understanding begin to emerge. Ecosystems have a history and exist independently of our noticing them.	Classrooms are not self-evident environments. We need to dig below surface impressions and assumptions to notice the complexity. All classroom situations have a history which make them what they are.
The developing teacher begins to appreciate more clearly the tensions which exist in classrooms and the part she or he plays in the making or breaking of a classroom environment.	• dynamic • fragile	Ecosystems teem with activity which results in constant interaction, constant change. Some find change more difficult than others. All have a fragility but the least adaptable are the most brittle.	Classrooms are dynamic environments with much happening and where change is constant. To appreciate this is to understand also that classrooms are fragile. Small events can trigger big changes.
As a result of deepening reflective experience the proficient teacher seeks to manage the parts which make up the balanced whole.	• parts and wholes • balanceefefefe	Without the concept of the ecosystem the parts of the natural world seem to exist and operate independently. Ecology has taught us to view the parts in relation to the whole, and to see the whole as striving for balance.	All classroom environments consists of many parts: students, furniture, teachers, equipment, and all are subject to external influence: time of day, previous lesson, weather. These parts make up the whole. It is in trying to maintain balance of all the various parts to the whole that we are best able to produce creative classroom environments.

Figure 4: *Classrooms as ecosystems – the analogy.*

Category	Near the start of the lesson	During the lesson	Around the end of the lesson
Not self-evident	What preparation – behind the scene work – has helped shape the environment as you perceive it?	How would you characterise the relationship between the teacher and students? How has this been achieved?	
Given	What established practices or procedures are evident?	List what you believe are the expectations which both teacher(s) and students have of each other. In what ways does this impact on the lesson?	
Dynamic	As students enter the room and 'settle down' observe the multitude of interactions occurring simultaneously. Can you categorise these?	All lessons have a dynamic, driven by the energy of the people in the classroom. To what degree has the energy been harnessed and directed? Are there common goals?	
Fragile	Can you identify anything which may lead this nearly formed classroom to fracture or to be disrupted? (How strong – or weak – does the classroom feel?)	Is there a destructive element in the dynamic of the classroom? Can you identify its source? What action, or characteristics of classroom management help accommodate or absorb this tendency?	
Parts and wholes	List the elements of this newly forming classroom which have required planning and preparation.	Make a list of all the separate parts that make up the whole of this 'classroom exercise'. Your list will range from the purely physical (e.g. learning materials, furniture, wall displays) to social (e.g. groupings of students, roles adopted by individuals, language used by teacher(s) and student(s)).	
Balance	What preparations or actions are designed to maintain or create balance?	Note that a lesson will usually have varying pace of rhythm and might have to accommodate unforeseen change. But does this lesson maintain balance? What are the characteristics of this?	

Figure 5: *Classrooms as ecosystems – the categories.*

On the other hand, the novice teacher found the long list of classroom characteristics produced could not easily be set back into their place in a holistic framework. She writes:

'For a novice, when the list of qualities becomes lengthy, the interplay between qualities, which is clearly at the heart of the system, is lost' and concludes *'I do think that I have improved (in classroom observation) and certainly the use of the ecosystem model has helped to guide my observation. Slowly the classroom is becoming a little less unfamiliar.'*

Classrooms are superficially familiar places - everyone, because they have attended school, believes that they know something about teaching. One of the key principles of teacher education at all levels is to find ways to analyse practice which reaches below the surface. Classrooms are more complex environments than they sometimes seem and it is this that the beginner, quoted above, seems to be learning. The interesting final phrase in the quotation above surely signals a novice geography teacher making good progress in her understanding of the complexity of classrooms.

Observing selected aspects of classrooms

Most observers focus on one or two aspects of classrooms because they have a particular agenda; an issue that needs looking into or a question that they feel may benefit from observational research. Teachers conduct small-scale research to answer questions of interest to their own work or to respond to the needs of a whole school. The Teacher Training Agency (TTA) has funded small-scale observational projects which can be viewed on its website (http://www.teach-tta.gov.uk). Busy teachers have often found a prepared, structured framework useful in organising their observations and the following structures are suggestions for observation focus. Frameworks devised or adapted by individual teachers are likely to yield more relevant and useful data than those adapted from an external source.

Behaviour management

What types of student misbehaviour occur and what strategies do teachers employ to deal with them? Figures 6 and 7 give examples of pro-formas that could be used to structure observations of students behaviour to answer this type of question.

Figure 6: *A pro-forma for use in observing disruptive behaviour.*

Name of observer: _____ School:_____

Date/time:_____ Class:_____

Type of disruptive behaviour	Tally of times observed (or comment if more appropriate)
Off task talking	
Answering back	
Disobeying teacher	
Making silly noises	
Inappropriate calling out/interrupting	
Having to borrow equipment	
Physical aggression	
Swearing/cursing	
Going out of seat at inappropriate time	
Insulting/arguing with teacher	
Insulting/arguing with other student	
Disobeying teacher instructions	
Other (state)	

Name of observer: _____ School:_____

Date/time:_____ Class:_____

Teacher's corrective action	Tally of times observed (or comment if more appropriate)
Facial expression	
Gesture	
Tactical ignoring	
Giving simple directions	
Positive reinforcement	
Re-statement of the rules	
Question and feedback	
Simple choice	
Isolation from peers	
Isolation from class (exit from room)	
Other (state)	

Figure 7: *A pro-forma for use with managing disruptive behaviour. Note: The terminology and method of use of these forms of corrective action are explained in Rogers, 1990.*

A more diagnostic and thought-provoking analysis could centre on the following questions:

- What behaviour is causing concern? Specify the behaviour clearly; do not merely re-label the student.
- In what situations does the behaviour occur? In what settings or contexts?
- In what situations does the behaviour not occur (this can often be the most illuminating question)?
- What happens before the behaviour? A precipitating pattern? A build up? A trigger?
- What follows it; something which maintains the behaviour?
- What skills does the student demonstrate? Social/communication skills? Learning/classroom skills?
- What skills does the student apparently not demonstrate? How may these be developed?
- What view does the student have of her behaviour? What does it mean to her?
- What view does the student have of himself? How may his behaviour enhance that view?
- What view do others have of the student? How has this developed? Is it self-fulfilling? Can it change?
- Who is most concerned by this behaviour? Adapted from Watkins, 1995.

Looking at behaviour and behaviour management in a variety of situations, e.g. whole class, group work and conversations between individuals, is also a useful extension of this type of work.

Beginnings and endings of lessons

Clearly planned and executed lesson beginnings are often the basis for a successful lesson and much can be learnt from studying them carefully. The following questions are useful:

- Were the children left outside until the teacher came or did they have entry without the teacher?
- Did they enter quietly, in silence or in what manner? Who decided this?
- Did the teacher stand at the door or did she get on with sorting out her own books and materials while the students came in?
- Do students have their own seats or do they sit anywhere? Is seating in groups, pairs or another arrangement?
- Did the teacher take the register? When? Did it disrupt, have no effect on or pacify the class?
- How many students did the teacher speak to before the lesson started? Was it public conversation or was it small group/single conversation? What was it about?
- At what point did the lesson begin? How do you know; what was the signal?
- Did students bring bags and coats into the lesson? What did they do with them? Who organised this?
- At what point did the students know what the lesson was about?
- How long did it take for the lesson proper to start? Adapted from: Turner, 1995.

Other questions can be created to focus studies on lesson endings, different episodes of lessons and transitions between episodes.

Teacher positioning within the classroom

The study of a teacher's movements in the classroom can be interesting and illuminating. Questions that focus observation work are:

- Where do teachers position themselves within the classroom during different episodes of a lesson?
- How do they move around the room?
- How do they help one student (group) and at the same time control the classroom?

Figure 8, opposite, shows one completed example. This diagram should form the basis for a discussion between observer and observed, focusing on questions such as:

- How much movement takes place and at what stages during the lesson?
- Do several students take up more of the teachers' time for individual help?
- Are resources and equipment ergonomically placed or could there be better arrangements?

In the interests of creating a 'natural' environment it may be a good idea to keep this observation from the teacher until the debriefing session. It would be difficult for teachers told of the focus not to be conscious of it, and therefore adapt their movements during the lesson.

Students' learning

- How effective is the learning process within the classroom?
- How can this be recognised?
- When and why does it *not* take place?

Teachers rarely have the time to concentrate on how and what individual students are learning because their classes usually have more than 25 students, all needing attention. Here the observer can focus on several students during a lesson or series of lessons, and study body language, motivation, response and production of work. A simple table could be constructed to structure this observation (see Figure 9).

The observer can discuss the learning that is taking place with the students. For example, 'Can you tell me what you're learning today?' 'Why do you think you are learning about the Kobe earthquake today?' Tape recordings of the responses are likely to be useful to the observer and to the teacher.

Figure 8: *A completed example of the movement of a teacher during one lesson. Note how few students are visited; of the ones who are, two are visited more than once, the introduction/ question and answer session from the front of the class takes up most of the teacher's time.*

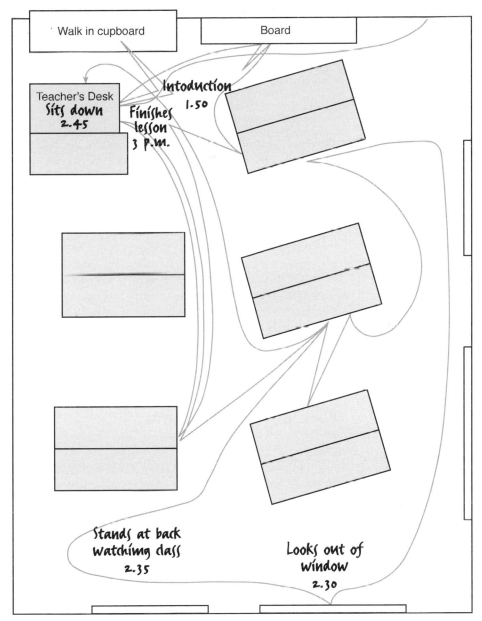

Equality of opportunity, equality of treatment

Are all students given fair treatment? Are girls/boys or more able/less able students achieving their full potential? Is there any group of students not receiving appropriate teaching? These questions are suitable foci for observers although they are not easy questions to answer.

Figure 9: *The extent of learning for Student A.*

Student A What is the student doing?	How is this contributing (or not) to meaningful learning?	What might be done to improve the learning process?
Whispering to her neighbour during teacher talk about characteristics of less developed countries at beginning of lesson.	Likely to miss key parts and require more assistance later.	Teacher to make sure everyone has pens down and is listening.
Spent over eight minutes copying out the simple diagram from the book before key labels have to be added.	Time wasted on activity where no learning was taking place.	Small diagrams pasted (by student) into book. Students need to carry glue sticks for this. School issue?

Pro-formas, such as that shown in Figure 10, can be created to give a structure to any enquiry where specific groups of students can be identified. In the example from King (1996, p. 17) the observer was attempting to find out if the teacher directed questions more often to girls than boys. In addition to producing the diagram, the observer noted that the girls more often sat towards the front of the class and that the teacher tended to favour asking students who were in his immediate line of vision. It was reported that boys and girls put up their hands to answer questions about the same number of times. Clearly this small-scale research and subsequent discussion provided valuable information to the teacher being observed.

Formative assessment

Observation can help teachers think more deeply about the use of assessment strategies. An understanding and using formative assessment is increasingly being recognised as essential for raising standards in classrooms. Formative assessment is that which is carried out as a normal part of everyday teaching and learning to provide detailed information about students' progress and attainment. This form of assessment helps teachers to plan future teaching and learning more effectively. Suitable questions here would be:

- How is work marked? Are there comments which students would find useful? Do the comments help to set targets and suggest ways of improving? Are books marked regularly? Do students respond through correcting spelling or finishing incomplete work?
- How do teachers ask questions? Are all students targeted? Are secondary questions asked to improve answers given?
- Are students encouraged to ask questions? If they do, how does the teacher respond?
- How does the teacher support students? Are only students who encounter problems supported or is the understanding of all students challenged?
- Does the teacher use some students' difficulties or best practice to spread learning across the whole class? Is the lesson plan flexible enough to allow for change?

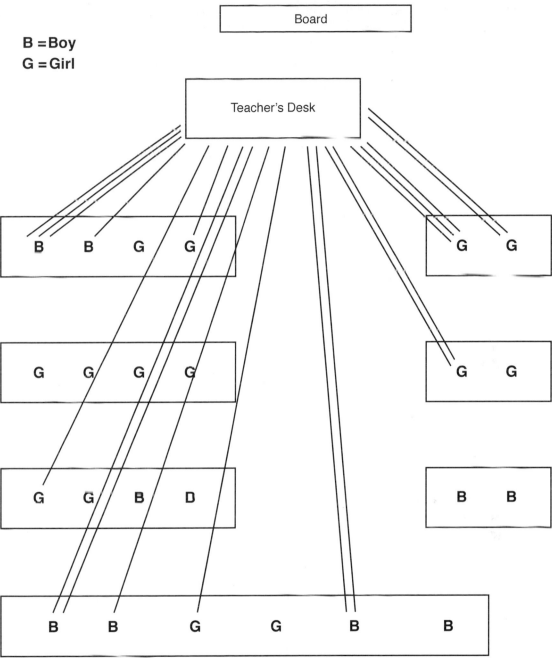

Figure 10:
A completed example of observation of teacher-directed questions.

An observation of this type will benefit from discussion with the teacher after the lesson. Starting points might be: How well did you feel that lesson worked? What did you feel about how much and how the students' worked? What did the students' responses tell you? The observer may then be able to feed in his or her thoughts to help the discussion develop.

Photo: Sheila King, Institute of Education.

3: Observing geography classrooms

The examples in Chapter 2 relate to any classroom and are therefore useful to *all* teachers who wish to observe. The following suggestions for observation foci relate to a variety of strategies and activities especially relevant to geography teachers and students.

Use of ICT

Information and communications technology (ICT) is increasingly used to enhance students' learning, and geography teachers have frequently taken a lead in delivering ICT across the curriculum. However, there are many teachers who feel threatened and hesitant about becoming involved. Observing and helping other teachers who work with computers (and camera and video) is a useful start to breaking down the barriers. Figure 11, overleaf, shows a range of questions which teachers need to consider when using ICT and which could form a frame for observation. Such observation is likely to be most useful when teachers begin to use the new technologies but could also be part of a departmental monitoring process.

Within the geography classroom, observations could also focus on concept and language acquisition, use of questioning techniques and students' oral participation.

Schemes of work

Schemes of work and their suggested teaching strategies inform class teachers about *what* geographical content and skills should be taught, but exactly how a teacher translates these into practice is often more difficult than it seems. Exploring the questions 'I can see what this lesson is *about* but what exactly is it *for*? Why is it being studied?' help to see the lesson framework in the wider context and can be a useful angle from which to look at lesson content. The case study in Figure 1 on page 12 shows how one newly-qualified teacher used observation work on glaciation to improve her understanding of teaching physical geography topics. It also demonstrates how a whole department can benefit if time is given to discussion and dissemination of the outcomes.

Resource management

Hardware: How many machines support the activity? Where are they? How are they utilised?

Software: Does it run? How much time would the teacher need to become familiar with it? Did it need setting up in advance?

Support: Is technical support available? Are there any support staff, novice teachers, sixth formers who may lend a hand? If so, how are they best utilised?

Classroom management

Is there an additional set of student management issues compared to other classrooms?
- Do students behave differently when using computers?
- Do they show more interest or motivation?
- How do I manage to support all students if the technology goes wrong?

Teaching and learning strategies

What geographical and what IT knowledge, understanding and skills are being learnt?

Is better learning taking place because ICT is used? Could the teacher have used other strategies equally well?

What preparation involving ICT needs to go on before the lesson?

How are students' instructions delivered? Online? Help sheets? By the teacher?

If the task is not completed in the time allowed how will it be taken forward?

Assessment

What are the assessment criteria? Are students aware of both the geographical criteria and the ICT criteria? Are students clear about these from the start?

At key stage 3 can work be assessed to feed into the geography assessment records and also into those for ICT?

Figure 11:
Questions for consideration when observing lessons involving ICT. Photo: Sheila Waddington.

Use of language

The use of language in classrooms in general is widely covered in the literature. For example, Stubbs (1983) and Edwards and Westgate (1987) address different types of classroom discourse. Writings within a geographical context include Butt (1997), Carter (1991) and Slater (1989). Butt argues that 'language' encompasses a huge variety of:

> *'talk, reading and writing that children undertake; the relationship between these activities and the process of learning; and the nature of the communication between the teacher and the learner'* (Butt, 1997, p. 154).

Since learning is closely associated with the comprehension and use of different forms of language, useful observations could be made which focus on this area. Some of the questions that could be used are:

- What types of question are being used by the teacher? (See Figure 12 for one classification.)
- Does the teacher use geographical terms in an informative but supportive way?
- Do the students use geographical terms with confidence? Are they encouraged to use such terms by the teacher?
- What strategies does the teacher use to encourage students' acquisition of new terms and vocabulary?
- Does the teacher demonstrate an awareness that students will sometimes find terms difficult to remember or understand?

One area of language that can be studied in most geography lessons is the teacher's questioning skills. The geography programmes of study and level descriptions contain explicit references to enquiry skills and geographical questions so we might assume that geography teachers and students should be good at asking and using questions. King (1999) argues that this is not always the case. The following questions could be used to focus an observation based on question and answer techniques.

- What types of question are used?
- Are they predominantly yes/no questions such as 'Is erosion likely to take place there?' 'Is the shopping centre near a main road?' or open/closed questions such as 'Why might people migrate into Phoenix?/How many people migrated into Phoenix?'
- Are secondary questions used?
- Do the teachers ask students to justify their answers?
- Do the questions tease out geographical information or are they restricted to general description and understanding?
- How does the teacher react to awkward silences? Is a second, simpler question posed? Are the students genuinely puzzled or simply lazy in answering?
- Does the teacher encourage students to ask the questions? If so, how is this achieved?
- Are most questions 'big' or 'little'? Little questions require short, simple, descriptive answers whereas big questions challenge more and require deeper, more complex answers.
- How does a teacher react when he or she does not know the answer?

Number	Question type	Explanation
1	A data recall question	Requires the student to remember facts, information without putting the information to use. *'What are the main crops in this country?'*
2	A naming question	Asks the student simply to name an event, process, phenomenon without showing insight into how it is linked to other factors. *'What do we call this process of coastal deposition?'*
3	An observation question	Asks students to describe what they see without attempting to explain it. *'What happened when the soil dried?'*
4	A control question	Involves the use of questions to modify students' behaviour rather than their learning. *'Will you sit down, John?'*
5	A pseudo-question	Is constructed to appear that the teacher will accept more than one response, but in fact s/he has clearly made up his/her mind that this is not so. *'Is this an integrated railway network, then?'*
6	A speculative question	Ask students to speculate about the outcome of a hypothetical situation. *'Imagine a world without trees, how would this affect our lives?'*
7	A reasoning question	Ask students to give reasons why certain things do or do not happen. *'What motivates these people to live so near a volcano?'*
8	An evaluation question	Is one which makes a student weigh up the pros and cons of a situation or argument. *'How strong is the case for a by-pass round this village?'*
9	A problem-solving question	Ask students to construct ways of finding out answers to questions. *'How can we measure the speed of the river here and compare it with lower down?'*

Figure 12:
A classification of questions. Source: Carter, 1991.

A further observation based on language could look at lessons that include debate, conversation and argument. Examples are: planning a case for or against the building of Heathrow's fifth air terminal to be presented at a mock public enquiry; writing and presenting the role of a coastal engineer during a lesson on coastal protection schemes, or running a simulation trade game where groups take on the role of an individual country. While the class teacher can rarely 'listen in' to a group with full attention or for long periods, an observer is able to concentrate on one group and study the quality of comment, which student(s) makes the best and the least contributions and why 'off task' talking begins to occur.

Lack of challenge

One Ofsted report, drawing on evidence from several years' inspections, saw the lack of challenge in many schools as an important issue and therefore one which may be tackled with the help of focused observation.

'Some teachers (at key stage 3) set undemanding activities ... and set tasks that were insufficiently challenging: students often worked happily at undemanding material ... Non-specialist teachers are increasingly asked to teach geography particularly at key stage 3 and one result may be that students are given 'safe' tasks which neither motivate or challenge students' intellectual abilities' (Ofsted, 1995, p. 10).

The extent to which teachers challenge students can be considered by observing existing practice.

Physical environment

A geography classroom and the departmental area gives students signals about the subject, about its ability to stimulate, to be relevant to their lives and to celebrate the work that they do. An observation can be developed to answer the question 'What makes a well presented, stimulating geography classroom?' Since students spend so much of their time in classrooms it is of interest to investigate what makes an attractive and instructive learning environment and whether students and teachers are in agreement about this! This can be researched through visiting empty geography classrooms with a suitable checklist. Figure 13 gives one such methodology.

An annotated sketch of various classroom walls and furniture is made and then for each item included in the sketch, the following features are considered:

Origin	• Other teachers, class teacher, commercial, other decorated, relevant to lesson, left over from previous lessons, information, e.g. fire exit, purpose not clear
Is it looked after?	• New, old, dusty, defaced, tatty and soiled (look for dates)
Attractively presented?	• Yes, no, care taken; colourful, eye catching. Have computers been used to produce display materials?
Been there ages?	• Yes, no, can't tell
Technical	• Name it, does it look used?
Made reference to?	• Yes, no, not sure
Noticeboard	• Does it have notices; recent/for students; for other teachers?
Safety/conduct	• Purpose clear, obscure; clear instructions
Language used	• Suitable for school use; recognises ESL or ESN students?

Geography specific content
- Is there a world map? A globe? Is there any indication of direction, e.g. a north arrow?
- Does the room indicate that geography is about places?
- Is geography shown as being relevant and 'up-to-date'? Are there news clippings or maps of places in the news?
- Is geography seen as an exciting subject from the displays?
- Are fieldwork and other subject-related events shown through photographs?
- Are there examples of practical work, e.g. contour maps, volcanoes?

The following questions help to make sense of what has been observed:
- Who 'owns' the classroom; who teaches there; how many different teachers use the room?
- What encouragement does the classroom environment gives to students (to look, read, engage, play, interact)?
- Are images of the cultural diversity of the school represented?
- How are the images of girls and boys portrayed?
- What value is given to students' work?
- Is this learning environment likely to have a positive effect on students?

Figure 13: *One method of evaluating the physical appearance of geography classrooms. Adapted from: Turner, 1995.*

Photo: Sheila King, Institute of Education.

4: Types of observer 4

This book is dedicated to a greater understanding of classrooms so that teachers can more effectively assist students to raise their standards of achievement. Perhaps because many schools now engage in staff appraisal and self-inspection, and their senior staff realise the value of this activity, there has been an increase in the number of schools that devise formal observation strategies as a means of school improvement. This chapter examines some of the reasons why experienced geography teachers may find themselves observing classrooms.

Observing classrooms as a geography mentor

'Mentor' here refers to any teacher or university tutor who has a responsibility for the professional development of a novice teacher. The quality of mentor support often has a huge influence on the novices' progress. Good mentoring can turn a proficient but complacent teacher into an excellent one or help someone who is struggling gain sufficient confidence and competence to lay the foundations for further progress. In relation to classroom observation, effective support includes setting clear foci for novice teachers' lesson observation schedules. McPartland (1995) offers advice to mentors on observation, feedback and review, and poses a number of questions for mentors to consider. These include times for the novice to observe other experienced teachers throughout their teaching placement, not just in the early weeks. Novice teachers should be encouraged to view geography classrooms both holistically, as with the ecosystem model (pages 20-23), and by focusing on aspects pertinent to the novice teacher's stage of development. Initially this may mean looking at the beginnings and endings of lessons, or at managing disruptive behaviour. Later observations may focus on formative assessment techniques or raising students' enquiry and thinking skills.

Some interesting and useful strategies which mentors may wish to adopt include:

Figure 14: *Novice teacher lesson observation schedule for a first teaching placement. Note: During the second placement, February to June, observation continues. The focus of each observation depends on individual targets and the need to move the novice teacher's work forward*

- Micro-teaching in front of fellow novices or a small group of students. This usually takes place at the beginning of the novice's teaching placement. A short episode can be taped on video and shown to the novice teacher to demonstrate important points. Suitable topics might be their university dissertation, a field trip they enjoyed or an explanation of a news issue.
- Paired observation where two novice teachers, or novice and mentor, jointly observe a lesson and then discuss points arising from it.
- The novice teacher prepares a lesson that the mentor then teaches.
- The teacher prepares a lesson that the novice then teaches.
- The mentor makes a video recording of a novice teacher's lesson and they later use a timetabled meeting to watch and discuss.
- The novice teacher makes a video recording of one of mentor's lessons and they later use a timetabled meeting to watch and discuss.

Name	School	Department
Date	**Observation type and focus**	**Outcomes**
	Induction week Observe a variety of different members of staff teaching. Focus on: a) The classroom as a whole b) Beginnings of lessons c) Shadowing a student through a whole day d) How teachers manage discipline	Feedback to school professional tutor along with other novice teachers during the weekly meeting. Be prepared to lead the discussion on one of the four foci (arranged in advance) In University feed this into workshop session following lecture on discipline and classroom management.
	Subject specific observation Observe two different geography teachers. Write down: a) all the geographical terms and concepts used within the lessons b) describe each teaching and learning strategy used by the teachers to put across knowledge, understanding, skills and values.	Report back to weekly meeting with the subject mentor and be prepared to use in University session on language and literacy.
	ICT based lesson Observe geography lesson which uses ICT to enhance learning. Use Figure 11 (or similar) as a prompt sheet.	Feedback to school professional tutor along with other novice teachers. Feedback into University session at a later date.
	Any focus on one aspect of classroom management or student learning (or other negotiated area). For example, how teachers use and misuse the use of questions in classrooms.	To be written up within the wider study of the chosen aspect and presented as part of the assessed coursework.

Photo: Sheila King, Institute of Education.

Figure 14 summarises one observation schedule for the first period of practical teaching. The novice teacher will be expected to follow this and be prepared to discuss it in follow-up sessions in school and at the training institution. During induction, novice teachers should observe the full range of teaching styles within the department, as well as in other subject areas.

Guidance for the induction of NQTs, (TTA 1999, paragraphs 45-47 and 50), emphasises that observation and feedback should be a key component of an induction monitoring and support programme. Observations should be completed 'at least once in any six to eight week period' and should focus on particular aspects, informed by the requirements for the satisfactory completion of the induction period and the NQT's own objectives for development. Reference is also made to involving other staff, within and outside the school, in additional observation work and in creating opportunities for NQTs to gather evidence to develop good practice in specific areas of teaching.

Using observations in school-based research

Recently, greater importance has been placed on school-based research. The TTA funds small-scale projects that are based in schools but linked to a higher education institution. Summaries of these projects can be found on the TTA website (http://www.teach-tta.gov .uk) Many professional development courses for teachers require participants to conduct school-based research as part of their assessed coursework. Some departments, perhaps without fully knowing it, engage in research methodology in order to answer a particular question. For example: How can we increase the numbers of girls taking A-level geography? How can boys' GCSE results be improved to the same level as girls?

The ideas presented here provide a framework which could be used to develop research on geography-related topics such as:

- Do students and teachers have the same views on what makes an interesting geography classroom?
- What can we learn from observing students on fieldwork?
- How do teachers use geography textbooks or photographs?
- In what ways does formative assessment in geography take place?
- How does geography contribute to key stage 3 students' numeracy skills?

Improving departmental standards through observation

More schools are now building regular and focused observations into their work. One school in west London introduced an observation process that began with Heads of Faculty observing their staff and feeding back general points for discussion at a faculty meeting. The second phase allowed every member of staff the opportunity to watch at least two lessons each year. Although the cost of supply cover to allow whole staff observations is high, this school has found it to be effective in raising the quality of teaching and learning.

One faculty head who found the experience especially useful commented:

> 'I had previously observed a colleague for the first time who delivered what I felt to be a good lesson. The teaching strategies employed, the arrangement of the room and the tasks were all appropriate. During the year I observed a number of lessons and saw the same limited strategies used in every lesson. It was only after a sustained period of observation that this colleague's lack of confidence in using a range of teaching and learning strategies could be identified and addressed.'

Figure 15: (opposite)

Ofsted pro-forma with guidance on completion of observation form. (For all subjects. Subject specific criteria to be added by individual inspectors.) Adapted from a guidance sheet issued by Brookbridge Education.

An increasing number of geography departments are including observations in their departmental action plans in order to address particular issues. For example, where a target is set as 'increasing the challenge for the most able students,' one or two colleagues might observe several geography lessons and report back to a departmental meeting along with some possible strategies for improvement.

With the introduction of the *National Standards for Subject Leaders* (TTA, 1998) and geography-related publications such as *Leading Geography: National standards for geography leaders in secondary schools* (GA, 1999), observation is likely to become a more strategic practice as leaders work to 'secure high-quality teaching, effective use of resources and improved standards of learning and achievement for all students' (TTA, 1998, p. 4).

Reg. Ofsted number		DfEE School No.		Observation type	L S O
Year group(s)		Grouping	A M G S B O	Present/NOR	
Subject codes		Accreditation	GC AL VA VI VF VP VO XO	Observation time	
Teacher's status	Q N T U S	Lesson type	CL RG IN MI XO	Support teacher/staff	

Context of the observation
- Brief summary of lesson content activities and organisation; role of support staff
- Details of work sample inspected
- Explain 'O' in type code box if necessary

Teaching
- Teacher's subject knowledge and knowledge of SATs, GCSE, A-level, GNVQ requirements
- Expectations (for full range of ability in class)
- Effective planning
- Methods and organisation to achieve lessons aims for all students
- Pace
- Class management and discipline (include group work if used)
- Use of time and resources
- Assessment (marking): use of assessment to modify teaching
- Checking for understanding
- Homework to reinforce/extend

Response
- Are students interested, engaged enthusiastic?
- Concentration (including when working individually and in groups); attentive to the teacher
- Behaviour (on entry, during lesson and on departure)
- Relationships with teacher and with other students (including those with different abilities, gender or ethnicity)
- Respect for feelings and belief of others

Initiative and taking responsibility

Attainment
- Overall in relation to end of key stage expectations (i.e. is level of work now right for a year group that will hit the target?). Target is national and school
- National curriculum attainment targets covered and level achieved where appropriate
- Skills/knowledge/understanding shown (what they can do)
- Any skills/knowledge/understanding weak?
- Literacy and development (if any) during lesson
- Number skills and use/development (if any)
- Note especially any variations in attainment by students of different gender or ethnicity or levels of ability

Progress
- Progress made during the lesson:
    Gains in knowledge, skills, understanding
   - Specific mastery of new material
- Progress made over time (evidence of books and other students' work) indicating how many seen

Other significant evidence
- Use of ICT and its level/quality
- Support for students with special educational needs (indicate whether statemented) by class teacher or support teacher
- Significant impact of accommodation, resources, timetable, etc
- Equal opportunities

Learning from Ofsted observations

Since 1992, Ofsted inspections have supplied teachers with a range of data relating to good teaching and learning. About 60 per cent of an inspector's time is spent observing in classrooms. Although teachers (and probably a good many inspectors), rarely feel that this amount of time is sufficient, what goes on in the classroom forms the key evidence upon which judgements are made. A pro-forma has to be completed for each lesson or part of a lesson observed. Figure 15 shows Brookbridge Inspection Group's example of the pro-forma with some ideas of what may be commented upon within each section. Although the structure of the pro-forma will have changed by the time this book is published, the content will be similar. These lesson observation forms are not seen by teachers or even sent to Ofsted but the evidence is used to inform the verbal feedback to individual geography teachers and departmental heads. It also forms the basis for the written paragraphs that form part of the full school report and are available for all schools from the Ofsted website (http://www.ofsted.gov.uk). Statistical data is collated and published in summary Ofsted documents (see Arnot *et al.*, 1998; Ofsted, 1999; Weston, 1999).

Geography teachers can make use of Ofsted feedback from lesson observations by using relevant phrases as action points for future target setting. Some hypothetical examples are:

- From an individual teacher's feedback
  'Your ability to engage and motivate students is good but students' progress often deteriorates towards the end of lessons when they have been left working too long on one task.'
  Action: Plan shorter episodes within lessons. Monitor student progress through work in class and exercise books.

- From feedback to a departmental head towards the end of the inspection
  'Students develop an understanding of place, themes and skills but much of the learning seen is teacher directed and students would benefit from being allowed to show initiative and take more responsibility for their work.'
  Action: Head of department to re-examine schemes of work for areas of strength and weakness. Departmental meeting to focus on areas for improvement and to suggest ways forward.

- Production of the paragraphs contained within the full school report
  'Students are making good progress at key stage 4 and above but less progress at key stage 3. Observations show that non-specialist teachers, used more frequently at key stage 3, rely heavily on textbooks rather than designing active and enquiry-based lessons.'
  Action: School standards fund money and half a staff training day to be spent on training non-specialists in the use of active methods of teaching geography. Department to monitor and advise on more effective time-tabling.

- National trends indicated in Ofsted publications
  'Often resources were of good quality but their limited quantity means shared books in class and prevents their use for homework ... The purchase of textbooks consumed much capitation, and many schools relied on a limited and sometimes limiting, single textbook series.' (Ofsted, 1995, p. 14).
  Action: Spend part of key stage 3 capitation on increasing and diversifying geography textbooks. Devise a strategy to do this over three years.

- *'The Geographical Association continues as a vigorous organisation promoting the subject in schools and providing in-service training opportunities, not least by its publications such as* **Teaching Geography***...'* (Ofsted, 1995, p. 27).
  Action: The department should become a member of the Geographical Association and the journal *Teaching Geography* made available to all geography teachers.

5: Using videos of lessons to practice observation

There are times when it might be preferable or necessary to use a video recording of a lesson in order to practise observation techniques. They could be used to focus on aspects of teaching and learning strategies or to study classroom and student management. Whereas more than one observer may be too many for a classroom, it is possible for a department or a cohort of geography novice teachers to watch a videotaped lesson. The tape can be stopped, re-wound and used to stimulate discussion, speculate about consequences or discuss outcomes. Useful foci might include: whether effective teaching and learning was taking place; how the teacher conducted the lesson beginning, episodes and ending; whether formative assessment took place; what the students were doing or how the resources were managed.

Of course the camera can focus only on one part of the classroom at a time and therefore it is not always possible to gain a holistic view. At times when the teacher is being filmed what are the students doing? Are they listening carefully, motivated by the lesson or are some daydreaming or finding another creative outlet for their actions? Can the level and quality of discussion ever be captured by the videotape? Students will react to the camera when they are aware that it is focusing upon them. Some students 'clam up' or become more cautious in their responses, while some become more dominant and 'show off'. Many teachers, when witnessing a heated, informed and fluent debate amongst a group of students, have wished they had a camera at hand to video that rewarding moment.

A video tape of a series of lessons accompanies this book. The lessons were filmed by teachers who were known to the students and who have a good understanding of classrooms. One advantage of this is that the students were likely to have been more comfortable in their presence than a professional crew. Some commercial videos available for observation work show students intimidated by the camera – they speak only when spoken to and sit woodenly in their desks, afraid to put up their hands. Hardly the norm for most schools!

Each lesson was one hour in length and the video has been edited for training needs. Each teacher has a different style of teaching. Two teachers were experienced heads of department, one a new head of department and one a teacher of only two years experience. The author wishes to thank those teachers who bravely allowed the camera to intrude their into classroom and for publication of the finished product.

Lesson 1: The Aswan High Dam – an example of a multi-purpose rivers scheme

Filmed by Gill Davidson, Tutor for Geography Education at Oxford Brookes University. Devised by Claire Rhodie, then Head of Geography, Broomfield School, Southgate. Year 10 (mixed ability). This lesson was the basis for an article by Davidson (1996) which applied Ofsted criteria to this quality lesson.

Lesson 2: An introduction to hydrology and the water cycle

Filmed by Sheila King, Lecturer in Education at the Institute of Education, University of London. Devised by Lisa Shufflebotham, Nower Hill High School, Harrow. Year 8 (mixed ability)

Lesson 3: Application of hydrology to the Amazon Basin

Filmed by Sheila King, Lecturer in Education at Institute of Education, University of London. Devised by Catherine Thomas, then at Nower Hill High School, Harrow. Year 8 (mixed ability)

Lesson 4: The location of a new coal mine - a group decision-making exercise

Filmed by Sheila King, Lecturer in Education at Institute of Education, University of London. Devised by John Mason, Nower Hill High School, Harrow. Year 10 (mixed ability)

Using the video material

After watching any of the lesson extracts, observers could focus on a number of aspects. Questions that might focus the discussion are:

- What evidence was there to suggest students learnt from the tasks?
- Were students challenged by the tasks?
- Did the teaching strategies seem appropriate for all the students?
- What tasks and activities allow for differentiated learning to take place?
- Was a variety of strategies used to create a range of learning opportunities? Were the resources and classroom management issues within the lesson handled effectively?
- Were the resources and classroom management issues within the lesson handled effectively?
- What was the status of questioning within the lesson?
- Was progression of knowledge, understanding and skills planned into the lesson?
- Was the lesson well structured to maintain challenge, motivation and pace?
- Was formative assessment used to identify students' strengths and needs? Was self-assessment encouraged?
- Were the lesson outcomes reviewed with the students and used to inform teaching and learning?
- Is this effective teaching? Justify your points.

The video can be purchased from: Classroom Observation Video, The Geography Administrator, Institute of Education, 20 Bedford Way, London WC1H OAL. Tel: 020 7612 6436. Up-to-date information can also be found on website: http://www.ioe.ac.uk/eeeg/

Bibliography

Acheson, K. and Gall, M. (1980) *Techniques in the Clinical Supervision of Teachers.* Longman: New York.

Adelman, C. and Walker, C. (1976) *A Guide to Classroom Observation.* London: Methuen.

Arnot, M., Gray, J., Ruddock, J. and Duveen, G. (1988) *Recent Research on Gender and Educational Performance.* London: HMSO.

Barber, M., Evans, A. and Johnson, M. (1995) *An Evaluation of the National Scheme of School Teacher Appraisal.* London: DfE.

Barnard, R. (1998) 'Classroom observation: some ethical implications', *Modern English Teacher,* 7, 4, pp.53-4.

Butt, G. (1997) 'Language and learning in geography' in Tilbury, D. and Williams, M. (eds) *Teaching and Learning Geography.* London: Routledge, pp. 154-67.

Carter, R. (ed) (1991) *Talking About Geography: The work of geography teachers in the national oracy project.* Sheffield: Geographical Association.

Davidson, G. (1996) 'Using Ofsted criteria to develop classroom practice', *Teaching Geography,* 21, 1, pp. 11-14.

Davis, L. (1985) 'Focusing on gender in educational research' in Burgess, R.G. (ed) *Field Methods in the Study of Education.* London: Falmer.

DfEE (1999) *Teachers Meeting the Challenge of Change – A technical consultation* (Green Paper). London: DfEE

Delamont, S. (1978) *Interaction in the Classroom.* London: Methuen.

Department of Education and Science (1991) *School Teacher Appraisal: A national framework.* London: DES.

Doyle, W. (1990) 'Learning the classroom environment: an ecological analysis', *Journal of Teacher Education,* 28, 6, pp. 51-5.

Edwards, A.D. and Westgate, D.P.G. (1987) *Investigating Classroom Talk.* Lewes: Falmer Press.

Geographical Association (1999) *Leading Geography: National standards for geography leaders in secondary schools.* Sheffield: Geographical Association.

Horne, H. and Pierce, A. (1996) *A Practical Guide to Staff Development and Appraisal.* London: Kogan Page.

Institute of Education (1999) *Secondary PGCE Subject Course Notes 1999-2000,* an unpublished guide for novice teachers and mentors.

Jackson, P.W. (1962) 'The way teaching is', *NEA Journal,* 54, pp. 10-13.

King, R.A. (1978) *All Things Bright and Beautiful?* Chichester: Wiley.

King, S. (1999) 'Using questions to promote learning', *Teaching Geography,* 24, 4, pp. 169-72.

King, S. (1996) *Classroom Observation.* University of London, Institute of Education.

Lambert, D. and Sankey, D. (1994) 'Classrooms as ecosystems', *Journal of Teacher Development,* 3, 3, pp. 175-81.

Leat, D. (1998) *Thinking Through Geography.* Cambridge: Chris Kington Publishing.

McPartland, M. (1995) 'On being a geography mentor', *Teaching Geography,* 20, 1, pp. 35-7.

Ofsted (1994) *Handbook for the Inspection of Schools.* London: HMSO.

Ofsted (1995) *Geography: A review of inspection findings 1993/4*. London: HMSO.

Ofsted (1999) *The Annual Report of Her Majesty's Chief Inspector of Schools 1997/8*. London: The Stationary Office.

Rogers, W. (1990) *You Know the Fair Rule*. Harlow: Longman.

Rowe, M.B. (1972) 'Wait time and rewards as instructional variables', paper presented at the National Association for Research in Science Teaching, Chicago, April.

Slater, F. (ed) (1989) *Language and Learning in the Teaching of Geography*. London: Routledge.

Smyth, J. (1991) *Teachers as Collaborative Learners*. Milton Keynes: Open University Press.

Stubbs, M. (1983) *Language, Schools and Classrooms* (second edition). London: Methuen.

Stubbs, M. and Delamount, S. (eds) (1976) *Explorations in Classroom Observation*. London: Wiley.

Tilstone, C. (1998) *Observing Teaching and Learning*. London: Fulton.

Teacher Training Agency (1998) *National Standards for Subject Leaders*. London: TTA.

TTA (1999) *The Induction Period for Newly Qualified Teachers*. (Circular 5/99). London: TTA.

TTA/Ofsted (1996) *Review of Headteacher and Teacher Appraisal (Summary of Evidence)*. London: TTA/Ofsted.

Turner, T. (1995) *Learning to Teach in the Secondary School*. London: Routledge.

University of Birmingham (1998a) *Observation of Students and Sharing Analysis of Classroom Practice*, an unpublished guide for novice teachers and mentors.

University of Birmingham (1998b) *Helping the Student to Observe You and Analyse Classroom Practice*, an unpublished guide for novice teachers and mentors.

Watkins, C. (1995) *School Behaviour, Viewpoint 3*, Institute of Education, London.

Weston, P. (1999) *Homework Learning from Practice*. London: The Stationary Office.

Wragg, E.C. (1984) *Classroom Teaching Skills*. London: Routledge.

Wragg, E.C. (1993) *Class Management*. London: Routledge.

Wragg, E.C. (1999) *An Introduction to Classroom Observation* (second edition). London: Routledge.

Wragg, E.C., Wikely, F.J., Wragg, C.M. and Haynes, G.S. (1996) *Teacher Appraisal Observed*. London: Routledge.

Contacts

Classroom Observation Video available from: The Geography Administrator, Institute of Education, 20 Bedford Way, London WC1H OAL. Tel: 020 7612 6436; website: http://www.ioe.ac.uk/eeeg/

Ofsted website: http://www.ofsted.gov.uk

For Teacher Training Agency-funded small-scale observational projects view the TTA website: http://www.teach-tta.gov.uk